WASHING RITUALS FROM BULGARIA

WASHING RITUALS
FROM BULGARIA

GEORGI MISHEV, PHD

PUBLISHED BY AVALONIA

WWW.AVALONIABOOKS.COM

PUBLISHED BY AVALONIA LTD

ISBN: 978-1-905297-72-6
PAPERBACK, SPRING 2022

WASHING RITUALS FROM BULGARIA
COPYRIGHT GEORGI MISHEV, 2021

COVER ART: HRISTO NEYKOV
ORIGINALLY PUBLISHED IN BULGARIAN AS Поливки. Ритуални измивания. София, 2020

DESIGNED AND PRODUCED BY AVALONIA LTD
BM AVALONIA, LONDON, WC1N 3XX, UNITED KINGDOM
WWW.AVALONIABOOKS.COM

British Library Cataloguing in Publication Data.
A catalogue record for this book is available from the British Library.

AUTHOR'S NOTES

This book contains an overview of magical spells and washing rituals using water from ethnographical records of the traditional folklore culture of the Balkan Peninsula, primarily Bulgaria. The practices themselves are reproduced here alongside details of their historical context.

Any reader uses the practices described at their own risk.

ABBREVIATIONS

- АЕИМ – Архив на етнографския институт с музей, гр. София (The Archive of the Institute of Ethnology and Folklore Studies, Sofia)
- ЕБНМ – Енциклопедия българска народна медицина. София, 1999. (The Encyclopaedia of Bulgarian Folk Medicine, Sofia, 1999)
- СбНУ – Сборник народни умотворения (The Folklore and Ethnography Collection)

TABLE OF CONTENTS

FOREWORD

BY IRINA SEDAKOVA, DR. SC.

Georgi Mishev, PhD, continues his work in *Washing Rituals from Bulgaria*, in which he presents his research on washing rituals and the use of water.

The fieldwork for Georgi is his personal life. From birth onwards, he learned from his grandmother Elena at her home in Bratsigovo, Pazardzhik Province, Bulgaria. In traditional communities, older relatives usually play a significant role in a child's development. Georgi had a close relationship with his grandmother, and she inspired in him a love of and a curiosity for authentic Bulgarian traditions, in both their archaic and traditional forms. The childhood fascination she impressed on him evolved into his passion, as well as his yearning to study, describe and cultivate herbs and other plants, and explore natural phenomena including mountains, springs, sunrises and sunsets, the changing days and nights, winter and summer. With the passing of years this love and curiosity developed into a professional interest. Georgi Mishev is an authentic gatherer and keeper of Bulgarian folk knowledge. Fittingly, this book starts with the memory of a story told by Elena to Georgi.

The interview he conducted with Mancho, the old man from a village in the Rhodope Mountains, included in this volume, is just a single grain of sand in the mountains of folklore heritage Georgi has gathered and preserved. Mishev has proven himself to be an exceptional authority on our folkloric traditions, rites, and language through his books, studies, reports, publications, and social discussions. He does not limit himself to the analysis of local Bulgarian ritual practices, he also attempts to uncover their origins, analyzing and comparing them with other ancient cultures, including Assyro-Babylonian, Thracian, Hellenic and Roman. His linguistic skills allow him to discover and access rare publications and research detailing the rites themselves and important background material illuminating their origins.

Mishev's systematic and scientific research methods, combined with practical knowledge of the traditions, ensure that his publications are always notable events. His work is not a *stylization* or *profanation* of the Bulgarian national spirit (or any other national tradition), frequently witnessed in print and digital publications; instead, it is a fine and exact scientific work.

In *Washing Rituals from Bulgaria*, Mishev examines water, one of the essential elements for human life. Humans cannot live without water; in this way, humans are similar both to the earth itself and to plants. Plants and trees need water to live and produce fruit; humans also need it to sustain life. However, we also need it for its other ontological properties – its hygienic, refreshing, and even aesthetic values. Observing flowing water is a pleasure; it is not by accident that the central squares of cities are frequently decorated with fountains. But in the folk culture still alive in Bulgarian villages, still familiar to many citizens, water is additionally deemed to have magical power. Such water has many names: we all know about living and dead water from the fairy tales; there is also untouched and undrunk water, silent water, water placed under the stars, and more.

Additionally, herbs and other objects may be placed into the water, amplifying their magical and purifying powers. Water washes away all evil and liberates the body and soul from the influence of the impure. Such properties of water are necessary for completing many rites successfully, and specifically for the healing practices explored in the present work.

This book presents an archaic worldview, preserved in the records of Bulgarian folklorists from the 19th century - but at the same time still at least partially alive in the beliefs and culture of the present day. As such, readers should not be surprised to read that diseases are attributed to mythological creatures as the *Zmey* or the *Samodiva*, or that they are caused by fear or the evil eye. They should also not be surprised by the folk belief that words have power. The descriptions of the rituals that Mishev has included in the text reveal a complex but beautiful worldview, conveying aspects of the richness of Bulgarian cultural and ritual heritage.

Works of research such as these, particularly those supported with authentic texts, belong to humanitarian science.

I am confident that this book will find its readership and, who knows, perhaps challenge some to study Bulgarian or Balkan folk traditions, or at the very least encourage them to show more consideration towards it.

Irina Sedakova, *Dr. Sc.Philologist, specialist in the field of Ethnolinguistics, sociolinguistics and folklore, Institute of Slavic Studies of the Russian Academy of Sciences, Russia, Moscow & author of the monograph Balkan Motifs in the Language and Culture of the Bulgarians: Birth and Fate*[1]

---

1 Балкански мотиви в езика и културата на българите: Раждане и съдба. София, 2013.

INTRODUCTION

There is no doubt that magic originated first in medicine...
Natam primum e medicina nemo dubitabit magiam

(Plin. Hist. Nat. XXX. I)

More than twenty years ago, I first heard my grandmother tell a story of how a washing ritual with a specially prepared infusion of herbs healed my mother after a long sickness. The story impressed me a lot at the time. The result of the washing was remarkable, and the manner in which it was executed was equally impressive.

The infusion was prescribed, with precise instructions, by an old woman from Selcha, a village in the Rhodope Mountains, who at that time (circa 1984) was a well-known healer and clairvoyant. Alongside her ability to predict the future, she advised people how to purify themselves from illnesses and other undesirable things. Many of her recommendations contained instructions for preparing different infusions, with which those seeking her help had to wash.

Over the following years, I encountered other examples and stories of similar washing rituals using specially prepared infusions, which resulted in the idea of collecting them into a dedicated work on the subject. Ritual washings can be undertaken for different reasons, but the primary purpose (evident in the reasons they are sought out) is the acquisition or improvement of health.

In striving for health, people from different cultures and ages have used a wide variety of practices to heal themselves and become healthy. In traditional cultures, sickness is not seen as a solely physiological event; it also has a supernatural aspect. Diseases were often attributed to external forces and influences of such mythological creatures as *samodiva* and *zmey*. That is why folk medicine applies ritualized healing methods that affect both the visible physical body and the invisible subtle part of a person and their surroundings.

Scholars of Bulgarian folk medicine's healing magic have explored different aspects of this topic and its ritual practices. The present work is however directed specifically to washing rituals, as I am fascinated by the techniques and their historical origins, through which they have been and remain a carrier of cultural information.

Before presenting and commenting on examples of healing practices, I would like first to consider some of these rituals in a historical context.

In ancient times, as in Bulgarian traditional folk culture today, disturbances in one's health are believed to be a consequence of the influence of supernatural forces. This is also true for most of the ancient world. Various methods were employed, in different places and periods, to eliminate unwanted external influences. Some practices were, however, almost universal – one example being ritual washing.

Though the thinking of ancient people might seem strange and abstract to us today, a significant proportion of their ritual acts were based on ideas and models which are apparent and quite close to physical realities and everyday life. Ancient people concluded that the best means to eliminate something that bothered them was to wash it away. This washing was considered equally valid as a remedy for visible physical dirt or pollution and subtle and invisible afflictions. It is out of this simple physical act of washing, through which humans eradicated dirt from their bodies that ritual washing evolved into rituals that everyone could use to purify themselves from impurities on a non-material level. However, to reach this state of metaphysical and mental purification, it was believed that the ritual washings had to be precise and extraordinary. Subsequent chapters will present several detailed examples.

Such rituals were prevalent as far back as the 1st millennium BCE, as attested in Assyro-Babylonian texts. They were known as *namburbi*[2] *rituals*, i.e. *releasing rituals*. Their purpose was to avert evil or other bad fortune from a person[3]. In some of these rituals one of the key methods for averting such negative external influences was washing with a liquid prepared explicitly for the purpose[4].

According to surviving records the liquid's base was mostly water with specific properties, and gathered either from a particular number of springs or from special locations such as sacred wells, sacred rivers or other specified sites. Once collected, the water would then be infused or saturated with purifying power by adding different materials of plant and/or mineral origin and by completing specific ritual acts. What

---

2 The present work uses the *namburbi* rituals from the edition of Maul, St. Zukunftsbewältigung, *Eine Untersuchung altorientalischen Denkens anhand der babylonisch-assyrischen Löserituale (Namburbi)*. Mainz am Rhein, 1994.

3 For their German name, the author of the cited study chooses their definition as rituals for overcoming the future - Zukunftsbewältigung.

4 For the holy water for purification, with which evil is washed away in the *namburbi* rituals, see Maul, St. Zukunftsbewältigung, *Eine Untersuchung altorientalischen Denkens anhand der babylonisch-assyrischen Löserituale (Namburbi)*. Mainz am Rhein, 1994, 41-46.

follows is an example of a recipe for the liquid to be used in a ritual washing:

> "…*take a vessel with holy water and put in it some gold, silver, iron, hulelu-stone, carnelian, lazurite, olive oil, extra virgin olive oil, refined olive oil, oil, the herb elkulla, juniper wood, cedar wood, tamarix, the herb that purifies (instead of it you can put the herb mastakal), sprouts from Phoenician palm and qan saleli, then you put [the water with] all these outside under the stars during the night."* [5]

These substances add additional sacredness to the water, as the ingredients were considered sacred to different deities, whose powers were through this added to the water. The liquid prepared in this way was believed to avert particular bad influences from a person through the deities' power. There are instances where the ritual descriptions include instructions for the stones placed in the water to be made into a necklace which could be worn for extra protection after the washing ritual.

The water would be further sanctified in subsequent parts of the ritual by uttering words over it, including the water in a sacrificial rite, or by placing it under the stars overnight.

Alongside the Mesopotamian examples, evidence for ritual washings can also be found in Hittite texts. These ancient Indo-European people lived in Asia Minor during the 2nd -1st millennium BCE, in regions which are now part of Turkey, Syria, Lebanon and Israel, and left many written sources. Hittite texts include numerous descriptions of ritual acts and information showing that separate ritual schools existed.

---

5 Maul, St. Zukunftsbewältigung, *Eine Untersuchung altorientalischen denkens anhand der babylonisch-assyrischen Löserituale (Namburbi).* Mainz am Rhein, 1994, 142.

Figure 1: an eagle-headed protective spirit holding a bucket for water for purification and cone used to be dipped in the bucket of water before being shaken in order to ritually purify a person or object.

An example of instructions for collecting water for ritual washing is found in a Hittite text from Kizzuwatna[6]. The Kizzuwatna Kingdom, dated to the 2nd millennium BCE, was once located near the modern-day Iskenderun Bay in Turkey. In this text, we read:

> *"When Palia, the King of the Kumans, places [the image of] the Storm-God, he makes the following incantation. He takes water from seven springs for purification of the town of Lavazantia. For the water of purification [he takes/gives]: 1 shekel of silver, 1 veil, 1 ball of worsted yarn, 1 tarpala from blue wool, 1 tarpala from red wool, 1 hakkunna-vessel of refined olive oil, 3 small flat loaves from damp flour and 1 jug of wine as sacrifice to the seven springs. When he returns with the water for purification, he takes one goose, 1 mulati-baked dish from half a handful of damp spelt flour, 5 flat loaves, a bit of olive oil and 1 measure of wine and all this is sacrificed for the water of purification."[7]*

These rituals also demonstrate the use of ritual washing to purify and release evil, including sicknesses, a practice which again is similar to the examples recorded in Mesopotamian texts. This similarity is likely due to cultural interactions resulting in the borrowing of ritual practices. However, it is equally likely that common mythological models and local characters would lead to similarities in the rite's technical nature.

---

6 See Strauß, R. *Reinigungsrituale aus Kizzuwatna. Ein Beitrag zur Erforschung hethitischer Ritualtradition und Kulturgeschichte.* Berlin/New York, 2006.

7 Strauß, R. *Reinigungsrituale aus Kizzuwatna. Ein Beitrag zur Erforschung hethitischer Ritualtradition und Kulturgeschichte.* Berlin/New York, 2006, 36-37.

"AZU-Priest or a pure woman takes a vessel of water or a kazzi-vessel of water and pours the water to the deities. He/she puts another vessel underneath and gathers the water from the washing of the images of the deities while saying: 'As this water is clean from all that is impure and as people wash magnificent clothes with it and it cleanses them from all that is impure, and as any tools are washed with it, and it cleans them from all that is impure and makes them clean, as this water liberates from all that is impure and makes everything clean, may the deities liberate you from all that is impure! You, deities, be free of evil deeds, from curses, damnation, from blood and tears shed, be thoroughly and completely free, and may the man for whom we make this rite be freed by you of all these things.'"

Then the vessel of water held is brought outside and given to another person. After that it is poured on the hands of the man for whom the rite is being carried out, from another vessel of water while saying: "Let all the evil deeds, curses, damnation, blood and tears shed, be washed away and may you, by the deities, be freed of them."[8]

We will now consider some of the significant elements in these rituals, including features seen in traditional folklore. First is the use of water from various places: from a spring, a well or a river. Sometimes the water is combined from two springs[9] or from seven[10] or another number, as well as drawing it from the spring several times.

---

8 Strauß, R. *Reinigungsrituale aus Kizzuwatna. Ein Beitrag zur Erforschung hethitischer Ritualtradition und Kulturgeschichte.* Berlin/New York, 2006, 342-343.

9 Haas, V. Materia *Magica et Medica Hethitica: Ein Beitrag Zur Heilkunde Im Alten Orient.* Berlin / New York, 2003, 144.

10 *"In the morning of the second day the storm god is washed with the seven pure waters."* Ibid. 144.

Figure 2: EFLATUN PINAR - Hittite Spring Sanctuary

Instructions for how to collect water is presented as a story of how the Goddess Ishtar went to the springs carrying an empty vessel without wearing her gown. Ishtar is wearing earrings in the shape of surasura-birds as well as a wreath on her head:

> *"She says to the springs, she says to the water springs, … […] she says to the deity of water: 'This water I came here for, please give it to me to purify the blood and curse, to purify the gate, to purify the [tongues] of the multi[tude], the curses, sins and fear!' [The spring] answers to Ishtar: 'Fill in water seven times and fill in water eight times, pour that water out and the water, that you pour in on the ninth time, this water fill in and take it!'"*[11]

Many additional components may be put in the water to strengthen its power, such as seven stones taken from the river

---

11 Ibid. 148.

in advance, as described in the ritual of the Amihatna priest[12], or parts of trees, herbs or other materials.

Another method for sanctifying the water is by pouring blood from a sacrificial animal into it, or by placing sacrificial gifts into it.[13] An example of sanctifying the water is the pouring into it the blood from two geese which have been sacrificed: the blood from the first goose is poured into the water when the moon is reflected in it, the blood from the second when the sun is reflected in it:

> *"The incense burner huprushi is lit up. The* LU*AZU-priest takes one goose and pours its blood into the water in which the moon reflects (during the night) in the name of Sarrimmati. Then he takes another goose and pours its blood in the water in which the sun (reflects) (during the day) in the name of Salus-Bitinhi. After he has poured out the blood from the geese, he puts some bread into the water over which he sprinkles some grout porridge by saying in Hurrian language: 'Imputte, Silaluhi, daughters of Tupkiya, this mirzi-dish, this offering, this round bread and these dulluzi, ... do not come by chance, but they are a offering for the water of purification!'"*

The next step, which is of great importance, is placing the vessel of water under the stars. This is stated as a requirement in the Hittite text, which says: *"And the water stays under the stars..."*[14, 15] The water is then used for sprinkling and washing.

---

12 Ibid. 148.

13 Ibid. 152-153.

14 Ibid. 153.

15 This ritual element is recognized and discussed as an ancient motive in an article, dedicated to this issue, by Крайенброк-Дукова, У. Някои антични мотиви в обредите и фолклора на балканските народи. // *Българска етнология* 1992/3. София, 47.

Ancient people treated water used for washing similarly to traditional cultures, ensuring that no one else stepped into the contaminated used water. In the Hittite rituals, this precaution has other variants, such as pouring the water from washing into a bull horn and then sealing it, as described in the ritual of Mastika (CTH 404.1):

> "Then the wise woman gives both participants in the rite a drink from a glass or bowl of water. Some sodium bicarbonate is put into it as well. Then both participants pour the water on their heads and wash their hands and eyes. After that the water is poured into a bull horn. The two participants seal it and the wise woman says: "Only when the former kings come back and inspect the country and the laws then this seal could be broken!".[16]

Water used for purification rituals must be disposed of at a place where no one steps. This is because stepping on water used for ritual washing leads to impurity and then sickness. A similar reference is found in Mesopotamian ritual tradition and texts:

> "When walking on the square, when Asalluhi was walking on the plaza, when he walked the street, when he crossed the street, [the priest-exorcist] stepped into the water poured out from washing and he contaminated his legs into the impure water."[17]

So far, I have briefly presented some of the basic considerations related to washing rituals, extracted from the source material available from ancient times, but these healing

---

16 Ibid. 157.
17 Емельянов, В. Ритуал в Древней Месопотамии. Санкт-Петербург, 2003, 233.

methods and their impact on the world, both around us and inside us, were not only known in ancient times.

ABOUT THE WASHINGS[18]

"Among our people, the Bulgarians, the practice of healing with washing – bathing in water with some herbs – is widespread. Therefore, I include one more recipe for a similar healing ritual reported to me by Mr. Dimitar Nikov, a teacher in the village of Bozhurluk, Svishtov District. The washing rituals are usually employed when someone has lain sick for a long time from unknown diseases, and the ill person bathes themselves or soaks in water with several herbs.

> *The following herbs are put in a cauldron with water at a full moon on the eve of Wednesday: spearmint (Mentha viridis), burning bush (Dictamnus albus), mountain mint (Calamintha officinalis), malva (Malva vulgaris), black henbane (Hyosciamus niger), tansy (Tanacetum vulgare), yellow sweet clover (Melilotus officinalis), walnut (Iuglans regia), mullein (Verbascum phlomoides) and cocklebur (Xanthium strumarium) and the cauldron is placed under the stars during the night. The cauldron is brought inside before dawn, the water warmed up together with the herbs, and the sick person doused with it while in a washtub. The water with which the sick person has been washed should be thrown away in the river or in a place where no man or animal steps."*

---

18 СбНУ, 21, Принос към българската народна ботаническа медицина, 58-59.

ABOUT THE HERBS USED FOR WASHING RITUALS[19]

"The herbs used for washing were to be picked only at certain times of the year, mainly in the week before Pentecost or on Midsummer's Day. The female healer would bless the water and sprinkle the herbs with holy water before it was used. The washing was then repeated - three times: for the first washing, the water was taken either from three fountains or from three wells for use; for the second washing from five fountains or wells; and for the third washing from seven.

The water was gathered in complete silence, without uttering a word, in the dark before dawn, before anyone else had the chance to take water from the place. The herbs were boiled in the water and the washing was completed either on the eve of Wednesday or on the eve of Saturday. The sick person should not wear any clothes. The washing was done after midnight at a crossroads at the first cock-crow with the following words:

"As Jesus Christ washed himself in Jordan River, thus may all evil and impure things be washed away from the sick person".

The water from the washing should be thrown away at a deserted place where no people could go."

REASONS FOR RITUAL WASHING

Washing, as a method of healing, was used in precisely-specified ways for certain illnesses and conditions. Primarily these were the so-called diseases that people believed were caused by supernatural creatures such as the forest nymphs, known in Bulgaria as the *samodiva,* or the Bulgarian dragon-like mythological creatures, the *zmey.* These were called "illnesses from outside". There were also illnesses without a determined reason described as unknown diseases. Likewise, the diseases or conditions thought to have been caused by magic or the evil

---

19 СбНУ, 21, Принос към българската народна ботаническа медицина, 61.

eye, which did not have physiological causes. Finally, in some cases, ritual washing was used as a means of treatment for issues usually treated by other methods, such as infertility, fear, fever, etc. Such separation of types of washings is conditional and - as will become obvious in some of the examples discussed - in many cases, it is possible to see common elements and the interaction of ritual patterns from one field of treatment into another.

I will begin with the most widespread washing rituals celebrated even in songs, namely the treatment with washing for releasing from the influence of a *zmey* or *samodiva*.

Figure 3: Zmey Loves A Maiden.

In the illustration above, the *zmey*, depicted as a flying young man, is whispering in the ears of a maiden. Only she can see him, she dreams about him and gets sick from the attraction between them.

An old woman is depicted next to the maiden, looking worried and trying to help.[20]

---

20 www.dolap.bg/wp-content/uploads/2017/01/N_Kojuharov-1922-Mene-me-
mamo-zmei-liuby.jpg

WASHINGS FOR DISEASES CAUSED BY *ZMEY* AND *SAMODIVA*

In Bulgarian folklore some creatures have been diminished to nothing more than a poetic shadow of their former selves. Once venerated by our ancestors, these beings are now remembered only as part of songs and fairy tales.

I will begin with the Balkan nymph. These beings are known to Bulgarians primarily as *samodiva* or *samovila*, by the Serbs as *vila* or *samovila*, by the Romanians as *ielele*, and by the Greeks as *nereids*. These beautiful mistresses of wildlife and rulers of springs, wander in the forests dancing gracefully, hovering over or under old trees.

Despite having different names and features, the samodivas are well known throughout the entire Bulgarian territory, as they all have some elements in common. For example, they love loneliness and do not like to be disturbed; they punish those who walk in the places where they dance their circle dance or where they eat their meals. They fall in love with mortals, but the object of their passionate love is in danger because an attachment to them is equal to death. And people had methods of treatment for all these problems. I will refer to them further on.

Following the *samodiva*, but not concerning power, is the frightful and mighty dragon-like creature called *zmey*. A lot has been written and said about the *zmey*, but even if modern people in the Balkans mix and confuse its image with the western dragon, the *zmey* has quite a different origin. Combined with its serpentine features such as scales, tail, etc., the *zmey* could take the appearance of a handsome young man or manifest as a pillar of fire in the sky - or only as a flame. According to the folklore of Bulgarians, Serbs, Romanians and other Balkan people the *zmey* can also fall in love with a maiden and desire to marry her. The consequences for the mortal are the same when this happens as for those who are loved by a *samodiva* – i.e. illness and/or death.

Before discussing the ritual acts developed as treatments, we must first consider the symptoms exhibited by people who sought the help of such healings. According to folk belief, the conditions caused by the love of a *zmey* or the influence of a *samodiva* have a lot in common. The diagnosis of the underlying medical causes should, of course, be left to medical specialists - though it is proper to point out here that in researches dedicated to the subject, those medical conditions are specified as psychotic disorders[21].

The negative impact that the *zmey* and the *samodiva* have on a person could be a result of their love (the *zmey* falls in love with a maid, the female *zmey* falls in love with a young man, the *samodiva* could also be attracted to and fall in love with a young man, or sometimes with a girl that she desires to take as a friend). It could, however also be the result of the *zmey* or *samodiva's* anger due to a violation of a prohibition or taboo.

---

21 Богданова, Л., А. Богданова. Любените от змей – душевно болни. // *ИЕИМ*, 14, 1974, 239-260.

One of the first consequences for the victims of this fatal supernatural attraction is believed to be that they start to languish, i.e. to lose weight[22]. They also become uncommunicative and alienated from other people:

"A maid with whom a zmey falls in love becomes alien from this world and its beauty, she is dead alive. The zmey neither lets her brush her hair, nor wash and change herself, etc."[23]

Moreover, it is believed that the *zmey* or *samodiva* do not allow their victims to find a lover among mortals. Furthermore, according to folk beliefs the *zmey* could be seen only by the person the *zmey* has fallen in love with - they do not tell other people what is happening to them and about their invisible companion because the supernatural force threatens them with death. Thus in some stories the female *zmey* says to the youth she has fallen in love with: *"If you utter a word I will not allow you to live!"*[24] The end of this state is usually death, i.e. the person who has been influenced by such a supernatural force merges with it after his/her death. According to the folklore belief those who suffer from the love of a *zmey* often take their own life.[25]

22 They are pale, yellow-green, cheerless and sorrowful, вж. Георгиева, Ив. Българска народна митология. София, 1993, 114.

23 Маринов, Д. Жива старина. Кн. 1, Русе, 1891, 33, цитирано и в Илиев, Ат. Растителното царство в народната поезия, обичаите, обредите и повериата на българите. // СбНУ 7. София, 1892, 372.

24 See № 340 Момче, любено от змеица в Мицева, Евг. Фолклор от Сакар. Част 1. Разказен фолклор. Сборник за народни умотворения и народопис. LXII. София, 2002, 264.

25 Георгиева, Ив. Българска народна митология. София, 1993, 116.

Figure 4: Samodiva, artwork by Georgi Mishev

Other symptoms could be visual or auditory hallucinations, epileptic or other faints, paralysis of different parts of the body (for instance of an arm or leg due to stepping on or touching a forbidden place, such as where *samodivas* had had their meal or where they danced), facial paralysis, and so on.

The necessary treatment consisted of washings with certain herbs prepared according to special ritual requirements to heal these conditions. The knowledge of these herbs and the way of their preparation was preserved in a number of folk songs. Typically, it is the supernatural force itself that reveals the appropriate ritual technique to the people.

This concept is shown in many songs and stories; in most of them, the youth or maid who is the object of the love asks the *zmey* or female *zmey* for advice under the pretext that they need help. For example for some cattle, a cow being infertile, or for one of their relatives. Consequently, the maiden Velika lies to the *zmey* by saying she wants to separate her sister from the Turkish man who loves her. The *zmey* then gives a prescription on how to prepare a herbal infusion to sprinkle in the yard so that the Turkish man will stop loving the sister:

> *The zmey spoke to Velika:*
> *– Velika, my look-a-like,*
> *go pick white gentian,*
> *the blue white gentian,*
> *gentian and yellow sweet clover,*
> *for those are herbs for separation.*
> *Boil them in a new pot,*

sprinkle them all around the yard,
only the place of the zmey do not sprinkle![26]

Some stories present the situation differently; for example, the *zmey* does not want to come close to a certain haystack because he smells the specific herbs that chase him away.[27]

Some of the herbs most often mentioned to influence the *zmey* are as follows: *Melilotus albus, Melilotus officinalis, Tanacetum vulgare, Gentiana cruciata, Gentiana lutea,*[28] *Gentiana pneumonanthe, Primula officinalis.*[29] For a *samodiva* the herbs mentioned are *Artemisia vulgaris* and *Artemisia absinthium, Adonis vernalis, Dictamnus albus, Veratrum lobelianum, Valeriana officinalis, Ajuga laxmannii,*[30] as well as sticks and straws from the nest of a stork or swallow.[31] Examples of such successful healings are praised in folklore songs:

"…Stoyanka spoke to her mother:
— Mother, dear old mother,
Gather all kind of herbs,
tansy and yellow sweet clover,
and single-stemmed cowslip primrose,
wash me with them
and may you mother cure me with them!
Her mother has gathered, has gathered,

---

26 Online: http://liternet.bg/folklor/sbornici/bnpp/baladi/11.htm

27 Мицева, Евг. Фолклор от Сакар. Част 1. Разказен фолклор. Сборник за народни умотворения и народопис. LXII. София, 2002, 264.

28 The great yellow gentian is called also shepherd's gentian and is used for the same reason, for which we find evidence in the words of Маринов, Д. Жива старина. Кн. 1, Русе, 1891, 34: *"But still the zmey are powerless against the magical power of the herbs tansy, melilot, iris and shepherd's gentian."*

29 Беновска-Събкова, М. Змеят в българския фолклор. София, 1995, 114.

30 *ЕБНМ*, 192, 91.

31 Тодорова-Пиргова, И. Баяния и магии. София, 2003, 328.

has gathered all kind of herbs,
has washed Stoyanka,
has cured Stoyanka…"[32]

Additionally, the herbs are used for protection. They could, for example, be worn in the clothes of the afflicted person. However, if the *samodiva* smells the herbs, she can trick the young person into throwing them away, leaving the youth helpless without the protection of the herbs and vulnerable to being killed:

"…– Son, my son,
come, your mother will gather for you,
from nine forests spring pheasant's eye,
from nine maiden's gardens
wormwood and tansy
and white sweet clover,
and sew them into your fur hat
and in your waist-belt…"[33]

The preparations of the herbs is connected with a series of ritual requirements. Specifically the herbs are to be boiled in a new ceramic pot, on a deserted fireplace (where the ritual washing could also take place),[34] on the eve of a Wednesday and/or a Saturday, in a deserted house.

---

32 Online: http://liternet.bg/folklor/sbornici/bnpp/baladi/13.htm

33 Шишков, Ст. Списание „Родопски напредък", III, 1905, 75. It is interesting in this case that the *zmey* is not afraid of the burning bush and the spring pheasant's eye, but even wears them as a gift from the beloved maiden, see Илиев, Ат. Растенията от българско фолклорно гледище. // *Списание на БАН*, кн. 18, 1919, 154. The *samodivas*, on the other hand, punish those who step on spring pheasant's eye, ibid.

34 *АЕИМ* 980 II, 9. Етнографски материали от с. Сакарци, събрал Рачко Попов, 1981 г. The washing ritual described there is made with an infusion from the herbs, that are left out after three carts of hay have been transferred. The ill person is taken to a desolate hearth, at which the ash is divided with a sieve. The record says that as an alternative to a desolate hearth, the washing ritual can be made at a field boundary, i.e. again at a borderline.

Figure 5: Tansy (Tanacetum Vulgare)

ABOUT THE DAYS SUITABLE FOR WASHINGS

"When you make a washing ritual for health, it should be made on a full moon, and when the washing is for magic, it should be after the full moon."[35]

"Only for washing, I observe to be made on Wednesday and Saturday."[36]

"Only when you make washing ritual for health it should be at a full moon, i.e. health to be full, not to be ruined."[37]

The washing ritual should be performed at a special place. Examples of these include a crossroad, a chopping block (for chopping wooden logs), a wheel dismantled from a wagon or a disassembled horse wagon. The chopping block symbolizes the cutting of the connection. Likewise, the wagon dismantled into parts represents separating those undergoing the washing from the supernatural force. Another suitable place is by the river; however, all the water from the washing must flow directly into the river and should not be splashed at the riverside, because if someone then steps on it, they will get sick.[38]

35 Тодорова-Пиргова, И. Баяния и магии. София, 2003, 44.
36 Ibid., 213.
37 Ibid., 303.
38 Тодорова-Пиргова, И. Баяния и магии. София, 2003, 330.

The combinations of herbs specified vary in different regions, but the herbs most frequently noted are sweet clover and gentian.

About throwing away the water from washings[39]

> *"Washings must be poured out in a river because if they are poured out on the road, they will then be transferred to someone else. If you pour out the washings on the road or another place where people pass by, then a bad thing happens to him/her: the cattle for work dies, a child becomes sick, a wife/husband dies, etc.".*

There could also be a requirement for the washing to be carried out in a specific order: first of all from head to toes, then from shoulder to shoulder on the back, i.e. in the shape of a crucifix, then the heart area, the knees, the elbow of a folded arm, the eyes, and finally the drinking of the water.[40]

The sequence presented in such ethnographical records is quite interesting because it represents an additional non-verbal code embedded in the rite. First, the person is influenced from the outside by washing, and then purified from the inside through the ritual drinking of the infusion.

> *"…the person tastes it, takes a sip from it, it is not a bad water, so that everything impure inside you may be cleansed."*

It is also sometimes a requirement that the water from the washing be gathered and poured out at a place where people

---

39 СбНУ 21, Материали по народната медицина в България, 64.
40 For the description of the whole practice see Тодорова-Пиргова, И. Баяния и магии. София, 2003, 328.

cannot go so that the disease cannot be transmitted to others. The belief is that the water from a washing ritual remains dangerous until it is illuminated by the sun - after that it is not a threat for anyone passing nearby.

These diverse elements of the ritual serves to separate the sick person from the cause of his or her sickness. The separation is accomplished by washing the ill person with herbs that make the *zmey*/*samodiva* unable to come close to them. In this sense, the purpose of the rite is to provide separation, but without inspiring hatred. Doing so is vital because provoking hatred from the supernatural entity could mean that the person would be exposed to its anger.

The elements of the ritual act induce the separation – the deserted fireplace and deserted house, i.e. the illness is to leave the person as these things too are deserted. The place of washing has the same meaning: the chopping block is where wood is cut, and the connection between the cause of the sickness and the sick one is to be broken, and the disassembled wheel or a wagon symbolizes separation just as the object has been separated into parts.

The procedure for healing diseases caused by *samodivas* is similar. The washings used in this case usually contain the same plants as specified above. Some suggest that the plants should only be picked on Midsummer's Day or that it should be from a wreath woven on that day. In this case, together with the basic herbs – gentian, tansy and yellow sweet clover – other herbs are used that people commonly call "samodivski", i.e. of the *samodiva*[41].

---

41 The epithet "samodiva's" is added to many plants – "samodiva's strawberries" is a name for common lady's mantle (Alchemilla vulgaris), "samodiva's candles" or "samodiva's distaff" for the great horsetail (Equisetum telmateia). See Козаров, П.

It is essential to point out that absolute ritual silence must be observed during the washings of people loved by a *zmey*. The ritual from start to finish should be completed without uttering a single word - starting with gathering the water through to infusing it with herbs, boiling it, pouring it, pouring out the impure water from the washing, and finally entering back into the house.

The main component in ritual washings employed to counter the influences of *samodiva* and *zmey* are three plants famous for this purpose. These are sweet yellow clover, tansy and gentian. Their ability to separate people from *zmey* and *samodiva* is praised in songs, thus transmitting this knowledge to a wide range of people in the community.

This belief that some herbs have a protective power is still alive today. For example, some years ago, during fieldwork I conducted in the Rhodope Mountains, a local healer shared his belief that if a person carries some sweet white clover on their person, nothing terrible will happen to that person.

Български народни название на растенията. София, 1925, 14, 32.

Figure 6: White sweet clover (Melilotus albus)

INTERVIEW WITH A HEALER FROM A VILLAGE IN THE RHODOPE MOUNTAINS[42]

This interview was conducted by Georgi Mishev (hereinafter referred to as GM) with Zafir Zafirov Manchov (hereinafter referred to as ZM), born in 1934 in the village of Kokorovo, Smolyan District. It was documented on the 6th May 2010, in the village of Momchilovtsi, Smolyan District. Also present at the interview was Iglika Mishkova from the Ethnographic Museum at the Institute of Ethnology and Folklore Studies at the Bulgarian Academy of Sciences.

GM – Do herbs dispel magic?

ZM – Yes, herbs can break it!

GM – Which herbs can break it?

ZM – I will tell you now what you need. You can ask me anything about water, about herbs, though, I can hardly speak now. Forty kinds of herbs are gathered on Midsummer Day!

GM – They should be different, right?

ZM – Right. Each third herb is a saint. And it is a sin to trample it, but it is not because we do not know that. Though they are saints and you gather 40 kinds of herbs, you take from the trees if you cannot gather so many herbs in one area. The trees are different. Each tree says something, as each herb does. And everything has a remedy, there is nothing that has no remedy, but we don't know this.

GM – You are right...

ZM – Yes, we don't know it. We trample on the remedy. Those herbs, when you gather 40 kinds, put them in a vessel. For some old rooted things and illnesses, even a priest, an imam,

---

42 Представеният тук текст е откъс, цялото интервю е публикувано в Мишев, Г. Антични следи в магически обреди от българските земи. София, 2015, 409-433.

could not help; a physician also cannot help. It is apparent that it is not for them.

GM – In what kind of vessel must they be put?

ZM – A big one. You take water from three places. From one side of the mountain, from the other, but not from just one area. Water passes different layers.

GM – From a spring - or could it be from a river instead?

ZM – Not from a river. It is dirty! The water from a spring is the most valuable, if possible. After the spring, it spreads and gathers impurities. Air, people, earth all make it impure.

GM – So, water must be from a spring?

ZM – Right, from a spring.

GM – From three springs, right?

ZM – Right, from three springs, from three sides. You put much water, soak the herbs, all together in the water.

GM – Do you boil it or just soak them?

ZM – Just soak them, do not place it on fire because they are holy ones, holy! And this water stays under a red rose.

GM – You mean the province rose?

ZM – Yes. The vessel with the herbs stays for one night. And only a fine kerchief is put over it so that they can take power from the stars...

GM – What colour must the kerchief be? Does it matter?

ZM – It is better to be white. White is holy.... Colours are also holy, and water is holy!

GM – And this is put under the stars?

ZM – You put it outside, and in the morning, you take it. All the sick people in the house should be washed with this water.

GM – Which part should they wash first – the face or what?

ZM – No, they must wash thoroughly in the bathroom first with tap water. They must be clean because holy water will touch them. And this holy water must not be poured into the sewers, but collected afterwards in a washtub or basin or something like that. One man should pour all over the body with holy water.

GM – And do you say something?

ZM – You make the sign of a cross, say a prayer to My God, Allah, or any other name you want, but He is one. He has 99 names and I can tell you all of them. It is enough to say "My God", no matter how you name it... Then slowly pour that water on the man. And you should not hurry up to dry with a towel. Discomfort comes out and someone could become anxious, something like anxiety. The power starts to struggle, and those herbs remove any impure things from the inside. The most appropriate time is at sunrise; the sun must be greeted by everyone, after that, you go to sleep. The sun brings health, luck and rich crops. We call some people useless, those who sleep in the morning when the sun has already risen. You cannot expect from them either work or health. And the washing is done in the morning. And you must dry the water from the body only when it starts to dry; we say it is for health. You start from the right side with the towel, then from down to up.

GM – So it can be lifted?

ZM – Completely lifted. Then you repeat it, but the towel must not have spent a night in the house, i.e. you take it tonight, and in the morning, you take it out and wipe the body. Sick people, let's say two persons – a man and a woman, a mother and a father, there is no matter, can wipe themselves and their towels must be wrapped separately in a paper or cloth and then brought to a crossroad where no one will pass by for 40 days. Even their relatives should not pass by because trouble sees you, we cannot see it, but the thing that caused the sickness to the person sees us. Thus it stays there. And when you leave it there, you must step back until it is no longer visible. You must not turn around because if you do you will take the trouble with you!

GM – *Are there any herbs for the evil eye?*

ZM – Yes, there are, but how to say, they are three kinds. They are against the devil...

GM – *What are their names?*

ZM – How to say, I know it, but I don't know their names. I remember only one of them - sweet clover, it has the white colour.

GM – *You mean the sweet white clover.*

ZM – So, when you carry it with you, you do not need to worry about lightning; the lightning will strike the devil instead. And the devil hides in a man, and if you have this plant, the devil cannot hide in you.

GM – *So, sweet white clover can help.*

ZM – The sweet white clover is the first one, I can name it, but the other... But if you have these herbs, you will not fear even thunder. The devil cannot come into you. It protects you from the devil.

GM – *Have you ever heard about samodivas?*

ZM – Yes, I've heard, but listen, I do not know much about them, but if those herbs are with you, no *samodiva* could impact you.

GM – *Yes, it could not. What about zmey?*

ZM – The same thing. See, we were shepherds and once someone told me about a place with big rocks, one big rock. And I was grazing the sheep there, and there were some watermills and the miller, an old man, told me once: "Come on, let's have a cigarette". I do not smoke, but I went, and he said: "Can you see this big rock, a shepherd, told me about a very beautiful maid coming out from there and if it sees a man, it will kill him.

Women's morals were very strict in the past. OK, but she was a real devil. He started playing the wooden flute, and she started to hum, and she went to him. He then became crazy and fell in love with her. They asked an old woman for help and she replied: "Son, why you don't eat, do you have any pain?", "Yes, I have", "What is your pain, son?", "When I grazed the sheep on this side, a very beautiful woman, a maid, comes out and I'm head over heels", "Keep away, son, she is called a Yuda[43], some kind of a devil, she will break you alive!" He doesn't know where she is, he falls in love with her. The old woman said: "Ask her when she appears, what is she afraid of?" He was playing the flute while shepherding, and she came, and he sat like me, on a meadow and made a clear place for her to sit. He told her to sit down, and she answered, "I will not sit.", "Are you afraid of something?", he asked her. "No, I'm not afraid of anything in this world." All was fine, but as he was clearing the place, the herb against the devil was there. He picked it up, and as he took it in his hands, she turned into a she-*zmey*. He destroyed her with the herb. And he thanked the old woman. So, it is good to listen to the advice of old people. There are many things that are exact and proven, and we should trust them and take advice from them. Now kids don't know anything. Now many things are not for a doctor. But a doctor prescribes medicine, which harms more, destroys the man, and worsens the condition rather than cures it.

It is important to note that plants defined as *belonging to the samodiva or the zmey* are put in the water for the ritual washing, i.e. they were deemed as devoted (or sacred) to the *zmey* or *samodiva*. However, at the same time, in particular ritual contexts, the same herbs are used to expel the spirits. This

---

[43] Yuda is a local name for samodiva used in some regions of Bulgaria - in the Rhodope Mountains and in Southwestern Bulgaria. The origin of this name, in spite of its sound which misleads to a connection with the Christian tradition and the image of Judas Iscariot, is derived from podyujhdam meaning 'to awake', 'to revive' from the Indo-European root *youdho – 'excitation', 'revival'.

illustrates that their use and that their power is not based on the principle that "the frankincense is chasing the devil" and therefore used for fumigation to chase away the spirits. Rather it shows how the power of the sacred plants can be used to subdue the supernatural power. Thus, by manipulating their holy plants, the *zmey* and *samodiva* could be influenced. Utilizing similar plants, called "*herbs of the samodiva*", a woman who wants to become a witch is washed and then initiated in service to those supernatural forces.[44]

---

44 See Мишев, Г. Началото на пътя на вещицата в българската традиционна култура. // *Балканский тезаурус: Начало*. Москва, 2015, 185.

WASHINGS FOR
UNKNOWN DISEASES,
THE EVIL EYE AND MAGIC

Other than the washing rituals to cure the diseases caused by *zmey* or *samodiva*, the second most used application for washing rituals were for healing diseases with unknown causes and/or long-lasting effects. These diseases were believed to have supernatural origins. Such diseases were said to include the impact of supernatural forces such as *zmey*, *samodiva*, the devil, the spirits of the dead, and actions taken against the ill person – including the use of black magic or the evil eye.

A familiar feature of the ritual acts used to treat these diseases is the preparation of the water previous discussed. The water is saturated with power in order to eliminate the disease from the sick person when it is used. However, as the cause of the disease here is unknown, the rituals tend to have a different emphasis. Instead of being ritually separated from the supernatural force (*zmey*, *samodiva*, etc.) the patient is separated from the disease itself. The rituals for this purpose employ different types of plants; specifically, herbs gathered from liminal spaces such as the boundaries of a field, etc.

In several examples of this kind of washing ritual, we find the use of the number 40, a number linked to purification and transformation since antiquity. For example, herbs were gathered from 40 field boundaries, or 40 different types of plants could be combined for use in the washing ritual.

Here again, the water should be "untouched, unspoken water", meaning that it should be ritually clean and not have been touched by anyone, either by mouth or by having words spoken over it. Furthermore, there is sometimes an additional requirement that the water is gathered from three fountains, three springs, or three other specified places. The number three is also often seen in magical rites: the words of the incantation should be said three times, the ritual acts implemented three times, and so on. Opinions differ as to why the number three is necessary. One suggestion is that it is symbolic of the three realms, i.e. underworld, earth, and heaven – with the belief that if the deeds and words of the ritual happen in all three worlds, then there can be no doubt that it will be successful.

A sieve is frequently used in these types of practices to pour the infusion through onto the sick person. Afterwards, the water from the washing must be disposed of outside. This can be done by pouring it into a river, at a crossroad or somewhere no one can set foot. The belief is that if the washing is done near a tree or if the used water is poured out onto its root, then the tree will fade away. This highlights the idea that the disease is transferred into the water, and will remain wherever it is poured out.

A WASHING RITUAL FOR HEALING A LONG SICKNESS[45]

"The following healing, using unknown herbs, has been recorded to be used in case of prolonged sickness or general weakness in children.

The healer starts by boiling a bag of herbs gathered from 40 fields. Next, they place a sieve over the vessel with water and leave it under the stars for the night. Before that, the head of a brood-hen who died on her eggs is first dipped in the water.[46] Then, in the morning before sunrise, the healer spreads a rug in the room and puts a washtub. Finally, the child stands up in the washtub. She puts the sieve over his head and pours out the water over the child, making sure the water does not spill outside of the rug. She then throws away the water in the river or at a crossroad while saying: "When these herbs go to their places, then this sickness could come back again."

Diseases caused by evil magic or the evil eye are healed in a similar manner. According to popular belief, magic and the evil eye are similar in origin and influence, but the magic is made on purpose and its power is stronger, while the evil eye is not always cast on purpose and its power is not so strong.

The diseases said to be caused by magic include conditions of general weakness or abrupt changes in physical state, such as intense intermittent headaches, dizziness etc. Diseases for which conventional medicine is unable to diagnose the causes; and unusual sicknesses. Evil eye diseases have similar symptoms such as an intense headache at the front of the head or forehead; anxiety and nervousness; high temperature; and

---

45 Родопи. Традиционна народна духовна и социалнонормативна култура. София, 1994, 74.

46 This is the so called *lehuso kokalche* ("a bone from a female died in child-birth"), i.e. a bone taken from an animal that died during childbirth, or in this case while laying eggs.

vomiting. These are all grounds for the belief that diseases do not always have an internal physical cause.. The folk believe that the condition should be treated with appropriate methods drawn from folk medicine. In addition to other healing methods, ritual washings are employed to cure the victims of magic or the evil eye. In such cases, the healing practices described for treating unknown diseases, and even for some of the diseases caused by *zmey* or *samodiva*, could be used, but with specific features added.

For healing the evil eye with washing, specific herbs are to be used, including some of the plants of the *zmey* like gentian[47], together with others such as silver cinquefoil[48] (*Potentilla argentea*).

Three examples of ritual washings to heal people afflicted by the evil eye or old rooted diseases follow.

47 *ЕБНМ*, 1011, 415.

48 This herb is used both for washings against the evil eye and for the healing of old sicknesses. Such diseases are: fever, headache, evil eye, stomach ache, see Ноев, П. Лекуване с билки. София, 1932, 63-64.

WASHING WITH HAWTHORN AND SILVER CINQUEFOIL[49]

"People follow the following ritual when a child is sick because of the evil eye or is sick for a long time. First, on the eve of a Wednesday following the first visible appearance of the new moon, they tie a red wool thread on the hawthorn and the silver cinquefoil; and a yellow thread to the child. Then, they break one egg in a green pot with some water over the head of the child, they put a black-handled knife and a red wool cloth over the pot and leave it outside under the stars for the night.

In the morning, they take the pot before sunrise, untie the yellow thread from the child, go and tie it to the hawthorn. They cut a twig from the hawthorn and a piece from the silver cinquefoil, untie the red thread and tie it on the child. Following this, they cut the red thread with the twigs and put it in a cauldron on the fireplace. Next they wash the child in the washtub with the water, with the egg and silver cinquefoil, pouring the mixture through a sieve. Finally, the water is poured out in the river or on a sapling so that no one can step on it."

---

49 СбНУ 21, Материали по народната медицина в България, 62.

HEALING OF OLD ROOTED DISEASES
WITH POTENTILLA ARGENTEA[50]

"Potentilla Argentea is used for healing old rooted past diseases. These diseases include fever, headache, evil eye, stomach ache, cramps, etc. To heal these diseases the following is done: 4-5 bunches of Potentilla argentea, including its roots, are boiled, in the evening, for about one hour in a clay vessel full of water. This boiled water is then left outside under the stars for the night. Next, the person is washed up to three times with the water. This is done on a Wednesday and a Saturday after the marketplace has closed, ensuring that the sickness will likewise end. The first and second washings should be done on a dark moon, while the third should be on a full moon."

WASHING WITH SILVER CINQUEFOIL
(POTENTILLA ARGENTEA)[51]

"Silver cinquefoil (Potentilla argentea) is used to wash children or elderly sick people when the marketplace has ended. Again this should be poured through a sieve with the person placed in a washtub standing on a rug. This water is then to be poured away in the river, and the rug washed. This washing ritual should be performed at a crossroad."

The ritual requirements for unspoken water used to complete the washing on the evening preceding Saturdays are also valid here. Nevertheless, there are also other variants where the phases of the moon should be observed. Examples include situations where the first and second washings are to be carried out "at the time of the empty moon" (probably

---

50 Ноев, П. Лекуване с билки. София, 1932, 64.
51 СбНУ 21, Материали по народната медицина в България, 34.

meaning the dark moon)[52], and the third washing at the full moon or *"on the eve of Saturday at a new moon"*[53].

The washing rituals used for healing evil magic may combine different elements in an effort to clear the negative impact of the magic. As discussed above, the water should meet specific requirements. These include gathering the water from an odd number of places (often 3, 5, 7 or even 9[54], and from various sources (for example springs, rivers, or wells, in different combinations); the water in each case remaining undrunk and unspoken. The water may then be mixed with a selection of plants, various in number and in type. One type of herb deemed to be especially strong for this purpose is meadowsweet (*Spirea filipendula*)[55].

A WASHING RITUAL FOR BREAKING MAGIC USING THE HERB SPIRAEA FILIPENDULA[56]

"For 40 mornings you must wash with the herb. You pour with the right hand and wash with the left, reciting as follows:

As the water is flowing away,
so the curse and the evil has to flow away!

Spatter the water to make it go a little bit upwards, dip some water out, wash with it, and slip the herb into the bosom (i.e. the herb that remains on the bottom of the vessel). At the end you go and throw the water in a place where the water flows fast and where a lot of people and cattle are going through. Say:

---

52 Ноев, П. Лекуване с билки. София, 1932, 64.
53 *ЕБНМ*, 1011, 415.
54 See also the practices for breaking presented in Тодорова-Пиргова, И. Баяния и магии. София, 2003, 484-487.
55 The plant is specified in Тодорова-Пиргова, И. Баяния и магии. София, 2003, 544.
56 Тодорова-Пиргова, И. Баяния и магии. София, 2003, 486.

As the water flows fast away,
so let the curse and the evil flow fast away from me
and let it go back to the evildoer!"

Several types of herbs are used only in view of their number, and therefore some other elements could be substituted: wax candles, lit up in the church with a prayer for health; a piece of the clothes of the sick person; incense; iron objects, etc.

A WASHING RITUAL FOR BREAKING MAGIC[57]

"To water gathered from three fountains, holy water must be added, as well as some blossoms from seven different flowers, three pieces of frankincense, three candles from a church lit up for health, and basil from the icon of the Mother of God. This is boiled and placed under the stars. In the morning the sick person is washed with the water, which has been

---

57 This ritual was shared by Elenka Sarafkova Misheva and recorded by Georgi Mishev. She was born in 1931, and was an elementary school graduate. According to her words this rite was told by an old woman from the village of Selcha in the Rhodope Mountain, who was a fortuneteller and a healer.

warmed up a bit. After the washing, the used water is gathered and poured out in the river together with the towel which has been used to wipe the man off."

In some cases, additional materials being put in the water might only be soaked, rather than boiled. This soaking, i.e. putting in the water without boiling, is something which would not be seen as an option for healing diseases caused by *samodiva* and *zmey*, nor for the healing of unknown diseases. The disposal of the water and the methods of carrying out the washing are however similar: the person washes with the water in the morning after the water has been left under the stars overnight, and the used water gathered and poured out at a place where no one steps - a river, a tree or another remote place.

WASHINGS FOR DIFFERENT DISEASES

As well as the cases of ritual washings as mentioned above used for healing, there are several other applications of this practice that can deal with particular illnesses in Bulgarian folk medicine. The treatment methods for them are similar to those used in the cases discussed above, as these diseases are similarly deemed to have been caused by external forces. For this reason, their impact can be eliminated by completing the correct ritual washing, thereby washing it away.

First of all, there is the healing of fear. Today the ritual incantations for fear continues to be practised as widespread healing rites, with minor regional variations. Some of these rituals are popular, and include practices such as lead pouring, incantations with using flour, etc. Others, including the ritual washings, are rarely encountered in the practices of folk healers. One of the most widely-used plants used in washing for fear is the herb maidenhair spleenwort (*Asplenium trichomanes*). This herb was given to people for ritual washing, as a herbal infusion, and placed under the fear-afflicted person's pillow.

Ethnographic records contain procedures for healing fear through washing rituals utilizing different combinations of herbs combined with fairly complex rites.

A WASHING RITUAL FOR HEALING FEAR[58]

"In the region of the town Sliven, there was an old man, Stoyan Yordanov Sabev. At 86 years old, he was living in the village of Zhelyo Voyvoda, and was very famous as a healer. Sick people from as far away as North Bulgaria used to ask him for help because his ritual baths, made with various herbs, was said to have helped many people suffering from all kinds of sickness. There was a time when it was commonplace to see more than 40 carts with sick people waiting outside Stoyan's house. He started working as a healer after 1927, after the death of his mother, who was also a prominent folk healer in the region. He used ritual baths, using the following procedure, to treat fear in more than 3000 patients

Stoyan gathered 41 species of herbs[59] including herbs such as burning bush[60], elecampane[61], valerian[62], lemon balm[63], coltsfoot[64], hart's-tongue[65], common toad flax[66], bathurst burr[67], male fern[68], St John's wort[69], cross gentian[70], wild tulip, and leaves from nine kinds of fruit trees – pear-tree, apple-tree, plum-tree, common toothwort[71] and others. He then boiled the herbs in water and placed the infusion in his garden under the stars.

As preparation for the herbal bath, the sick person was instructed to undress, and then the herbal infusion was then poured over them. The baths were performed early on Wednesdays and Fridays mornings, about

---

58 Янакиева, Ж. Народното лечение в Сливенския край. Сливен, 1980, 4-5.
59 The identification of the herbs is my suggestion, because in the ethnographical record some of the names of some of the herbs mentioned are unclear.
60 Dictamnus albus.
61 Inula helenium.
62 Valeriana officinalis.
63 Melissa officinalis.
64 Tussilago farfara.
65 Phyllitis scolopendra.
66 Linaria vulgaris.
67 Xanthium spinosum.
68 Dryopteris felix-mas.
69 Hypericum perforatum.
70 Gentiana cruciate.
71 Lathraea squamaria.

5-6 o'clock, and also in the evenings at about 9 o'clock. During the bath old Stoyan used to recite the following incantation:

> Evil hour, evil harm,
> Mother of God has gathered them all,
> Seventy-seven, different faiths (i.e. spirits)
> unbaptized, unanointed (i.e. unblessed),
> go there where there is nothing to eat,
> and nothing to drink,
> where there is also nothing good:
> Mother of God has brought them into the church,
> has sorted them out into various kinds and
> has set them free into the woods and
> has set them free as the she-wolf sets her wolf-cubs free.

His patients then waited 20 days to find out if the bath had helped. At this point, the old Stoyan would perform a second herbal bath for the patient for which different magical objects were utilized. The items used included: the hub from a horse's cart, the skull of a wolf and the horn from a snake. These objects were placed on the sick person's head while the healer poured the herbal infusion over them. Finally, the water used in the herbal bath was collected in a vessel and thrown away in a place nobody steps.

In these instances, an incantation was also used and combined with other elements, including animal parts such as a wolf skull or snake horn[72]. In addition, the washing was performed on specific days of the week, Wednesdays being especially suitable, as well as particular times of the day. In this instance it was done before sunrise, the idea being that as the sun rises, the sick person will also rise (i.e.recover) from their illness."

---

72 A horn from horned viper (Vipera ammodytes).

A WASHING RITUAL TO TREAT INFERTILITY

Another sickness that people sought to treat with washing rituals was infertility. According to the prevalent folk belief infertility could be caused by magical bindings. To break this kind of magic and to unbind the victim, specific herbs are used. The most frequently used herbs are the same plants well-known for treating diseases caused by the samodiva and zmey, such as gentian, tansy, etc.

If the cause of infertility is known to be something else, including something physical, then there are other healing practices, including ritual washings, for the purpose:

> "with water gathered from nine fords, seafoam, foam from the paddle of a left watermill, herbs and stones from the eaves of three end houses. All this is put under the stars and in the morning the infertile woman is washed with it, during which she had to sit on the hub of the horse cart."[73]

These healings are similar in appearance to the ritual for separation from a *zmey* as it was thought that he was one of the ultimate causes of a woman's inability to have children. A man could be healed similarly, and one of the most popular herbs against *zmeys* was sweet yellow clover, such as used in this example:

> "The herb is boiled in a copper vessel, only on Saturdays, and then the vessel is covered with the shirt of the sick person. At midnight ("in the dead hour of the night", i.e. around 3 a.m.) the water from the copper vessel is poured on the head of the sick person (at a trickle) in total silence.

---

73 Странджа. Материална и духовна култура. София, 1996, 218.

*The remaining infusion is brought out early in the morning
and is poured out into a river."*[74]

A WASHING RITUAL TO TREAT EPILEPSY AND FEVER

Epilepsy and fever were also sometimes treated with washing rituals. The washing ritual for treating epilepsy the same herbs for diseases caused by *zmey* are used, together with a strip of leather from the mouth of a wolf. This is a fascinating choice as the narrow strip of skin from the wolf's muzzle is well known to all southern Slavic people and probably originates in the oldest layers of Balkan folklore.[75]

The other elements in the rite are the same as those mentioned previously, the infusion is left under the stars, the washing is performed in the morning, the used water is thrown away at a place where no one sets foot.

WASHING FOR CHILDHOOD DISEASES[76]

"To treat a childhood disease such as epilepsy or fainting, the child must be kept away from roads where cars pass by for forty days. The child must also wear the same clothes for forty days. Then on the fortieth day the healer should collect water from a watermill, a whirlpool, a well, a fountain, a gulch, and a marsh. After that, they must dismantle a horse's

---

74 Илиев, Ат. Растенията от българско фолклорно гледище. // *Списание на БАН*, кн. 18, 1919, 157.

75 There are many publications on that subject, see Plas, P. The songs of the Vučari: Relations between text and ritual-mythological context. // *Slavica Gandensia* 26. Gent, 1999, 85–116; Plas, P. Falling Sickness, Descending Wolf: Some Notes on Popular Etymology, Symptomatology, and 'Predicate Synonymy' in Western Balkan Slavic Folk Tradition. // *Zeitschrift für Slawistik* 49.3. Potsdam, 2004, 253–72; Plas, P. Wolf texts' in Western Balkan Slavic folk tradition: outlines of an ethnolinguistic/ethnopoetic inquiry. // *Slavica Gandensia* 30. Gent, 2006, 77–88; Mencej, M. Funkcija gospodarja volkov v povedkah, zagovorih, verovanjih in šegah. // *Etnolog številka* 10. Ljubljana, 2000, 163–178; Ненов, Н. Вълчарите. Лекуване с вълча паст. // *Етър. Етноложки изследвания* IV. Габрово, 2002, 69–78.

76 СбНУ 21, Материали по народната медицина в България, 10.

cart. Then, in the middle, through the hole where the wedge was removed, they should pour out the water three times, before taking the water and giving some of it to the child to drink. The rest is used to perform a washing with the child at a crossroads.

Next, a bunch of cuttings from a dog rose plant is wrapped and tied with a red thread to form a large wreath. After being washed at the crossroads, the child is instructed to pass through the dog rose wreath; and finally the clothes and the wreath are taken to the place where the dog rose was picked. If the bunch of the dog rose is thick, then it must be divided in two."

The above examples for ritual washing for healing do not present all the variants by which this rite is known and used. The purpose here has been to present the role of this ritual act and its use in Bulgarian folk healing of children and adults.

A WASHING RITUAL FOR CALMING A CHILD AND CASTING AWAY A CRY[77]

"If a baby or small child cries and cannot fall asleep at the same time each night, its mother could perform a washing ritual to cast out its crying. To do this, she must go to three crossroads. At the first, she should take earth while saying "I take sleep with me!"; at the second she must take a stone and say "I take peace with me!"; from the third she should take some dirt and say "I take kindness with me!". She should then take these three things home with her, and place it – with three lumps of sugar – under the child's pillow for the night and let the child sleep on it. The next morning, the mother should wake up before sunrise and take the items from under the child's pilllow, adding three more lumps of sugar and say:

---

77 СбНУ 21, Материали по народната медицина в България, 39-40.

"I leave peace, kindness and sleep to the child and all evil, insomnia and sickness I will throw away on the crossroad!"

Next she has to return everything she took back to the three crossroads she took it from.

In the evening, she has to place a cauldron with water near the fireplace together with a black-handed knife, covering it with a red cloth. The next morning, she has to wake up early and remove the chain used for hanging the pot from the pot, and head it in the fire until it is red hot. The chain should then be quenched in the cauldron of water while saying:

"All evil existing in the head and heart of the child (she says its name) I put out to make it at ease and fall asleep as a lamb!"

The mother then washes the child with the water, as well as giving the child some of the water to drink."

CONCLUSION

Based on the practices described in this book it is possible to make some of the following conclusions about washing rituals.

Firstly, washing rituals as a form of healing ritual, has archaic origins. This is illustrated by the typological similarities it has with historical rituals from ancient times. These are some of the fundamentals they share in common:

- the water for washing rituals is taken from several water sources (a spring, a river, a well, etc.)
- different compounds are added to the water with the intention of making the water more sacred. These include herbs, minerals, animal parts, etc.
- the role of words is important, both the uttering of a special incantations and keeping ritual silence;
- the vessel with the prepared water (infusion or concoction) must be placed outside under the stars;
- the soiled water used for washing must be gathered afterwards, and should always be carefully disposed of.

Washing rituals are complex rites requiring the practitioner to have profound knowledge of a number of topics, most often including:

- the different plants and their relationship to the supernatural, i.e. which plants to which such forces may be devoted;

- calendar periods, especially those indicating the periods during which the plants should be picked or when the plant could be found, as well as when it is appropriate to do so, according to mythological beliefs;

- the correct manner in which to gather the herbs, and the performance of appropriate rites while doing so, so the plants will be most effective when used for the purpose for which they were gathered;

- the different kinds of water that will be used for washings, i.e. water taken from a certain number of springs, wells, rivers and other water sources.

- the periods which are suitable for the preparation of water for the washing; which may include the dead of night, before sunrise, on the eve of particular days of the week that are connected with particular mythological beliefs, etc.;

- the use of additional magical elements such as animal parts (example the skull of a wolf or a dog) or other objects which can be used, such as for example a sieve, iron objects, etc.

- the specific words to be uttered when performing the washing or respectfully keeping ritual silence;

- the place where the washing is made – at a deserted fireplace, at a crossroad, at the chopping log, near a tree, etc.

- what should happen to the water after it was used in a washing ritual, for example where it should be disposed of.

- the appropriate behaviour to instruct the sick person to follow after the washing is concluded, for example they should not turn back, should remain silent, must return to where they came from on a different path, etc.

All these elements are part of what makes the washing rituals so important for research, with the aim that the cultures in which they exist be better comprehended.

Due to the intricate character of the folk knowledge required as the basis for washing rituals, they are used quite rarely by the folk healers. Likewise, the songs which are sung to counter the love of the *zmey* and the herbs required for their washing rituals are not as popular today as other folk songs connected with subjects like marriage, family and so on. Furthermore, the typical member of the current generation is unlikely to possess folk knowledge about the traditional mythological images as *zmey*, *samodiva* and others. Most modern people are likely to be limited in their knowledge about the samodiva and are only aware about some poetic motifs connected with them rather than about ritual ones. No doubt modern ways of living and the modernization of society generally have played their role in this. Another factor is the development of conventional medicine and its achievements. There are however some fields, such as the healing of fear, for which a satisfactory therapy is still lacking, and it is for these kinds of purposes that folk medicine continues to be sought after today. It is in such instances that the washing rituals, in my opinion, continue in one of its most impressive and archaic expressions.

BIBLIOGRAPHY

IN LATIN SCRIPT:

Haas, V. Materia Magica et Medica Hethitica: Ein Beitrag Zur Heilkunde Im Alten Orient. Berlin / New York, 2003.

Maul, St. Zukunftsbewältigung. Eine Untersuchung altorientalischen Denkens anhand der babylonisch-assyrischen Löserituale (Namburbi). Mainz am Rhein, 1994.

Mencej, M. Funkcija gospodarja volkov v povedkah, zagovorih, verovanjih in šegah. // *Etnolog številka* 10. Ljubljana, 2000, 163–178.

Plas, P. Falling Sickness, Descending Wolf: Some Notes on Popular Etymology, Symptomatology, and 'Predicate Synonymy' in Western Balkan Slavic Folk Tradition. // *Zeitschrift für Slawistik* 49.3. Potsdam, 2004, 253–72.

Plas, P. The songs of the Vučari: Relations between text and ritual-mythological context. // *Slavica Gandensia* 26. Gent, 1999, 85–116.

Plas, P. Wolf Texts in Western Balkan Slavic folk tradition: outlines of an ethnolinguistic/ethnopoetic inquiry. // *Slavica Gandensia* 30. Gent, 2006, 77–88.

Strauß, R. Reinigungsrituale aus Kizzuwatna. Ein Beitrag zur Erforschung hethitischer Ritualtradition und Kulturgeschichte. Berlin/New York, 2006.

IN CYRILLIC SCRIPT:

Беновска-Събкова, М. Змеят в българския фолклор. София, 1995.

Богданова, Л., А. Богданова. Любените от змей – душевно болни. // *ИЕИМ*, 14, 1974, 239-260.

Георгиева, Ив. Българска народна митология. София, 1993.

Дукова, У. Някои антични мотиви в обредите и фолклора на балканските народи. // *Българска етнология* 1992/3. София, 43-48.

Емельянов, В. Ритуал в Древней Месопотамии. Санкт-Петербург, 2003.

Илиев, Ат. Растенията от българско фолклорно гледище. // *Списание на БАН*, кн. 18, 1919.

Илиев, Ат. Растителното царство в народната поезия, обичаите, обредите и поверията на българите. // *СбНУ* 7. София, 1892.

Козаров, П. Български народни название на растенията. София, 1925.

Маринов, Д. Жива старина. Кн. 1, Русе, 1891.

Мицева, Евг. Фолклор от Сакар. Част 1. Разказен фолклор. Сборник за народни умотворения и народопис. LXII. София, 2002.

Мишев, Г. Антични следи в магически обреди от българските земи. София, 2015.

Мишев, Г. Началото на пътя на вещицата в българската традиционна култура. // *Балканский тезаурус: Начало*. Москва, 2015, 179-188.

Ненов, Н. Вълчарите. Лекуване с вълча паст. // *Етър. Етноложки изследвания* IV. Габрово, 2002.

Ноев, П. Лекуване с билки. София, 1932.

Родопи. Традиционна народна духовна и социалнонормативна култура. София, 1994.

СбНУ 21, Материали по народната медицина в България. София, 1905.

Седакова, И. Балкански мотиви в езика и културата на българите: Раждане и съдба. София, 2013.

Странджа. Материална и духовна култура. София, 1996.

Тодорова-Пиргова, И. Баяния и магии. София, 2003.

Шишков, Ст. Списание „Родопски напредък", III, 1905.

Янакиева, Ж. Народното лечение в Сливенския край. Сливен, 1980.

INDEX

www.avaloniabooks.com

CPSIA information can be obtained
at www.ICGtesting.com
Printed in the USA
JSHW021621230523
42057JS00004B/165